JN102659

Talking About Our Campus

映像で巡る海外のキャンパス

◆

小笠原 真司

◆

奥田 阿子

◆

COLLINS William

◆

廣江　顕

◆

木戸 康人

◆

EIHŌSHA

音声ファイルのダウンロード方法

英宝社ホームページ（http://www.eihosha.co.jp/）の
「テキスト音声ダウンロード」バナーをクリックすると、
音声ファイルダウンロードページにアクセスできます。

はじめに

　長年英語の授業を担当していて、大学生から「英語の映画を字幕なしで楽しみたい」、「英語ニュースを聞き取れるようになりたい」、あるいは、「英語を国際語として使えるようになりたい」等の意見をよく聞きます。本書はそのような能力の養成のための、現地取材の動画を使用した DVD 教材です。DVD を利用したリスニング練習から始め、スピーキング、ライティング、さらにリーディングの活動を行い、4技能をバランスよく訓練できるよう工夫されています。本書の特徴をまとめると、次のようになります。

1. 英国や合衆国での現地取材の Authentic なリスニング活動のための DVD
2. リスニングから始めて、4技能を鍛える統合型の教材
3. リスニング活動ではステップごとにタスクが用意され、意識的にトップダウンによる処理方法が身につけられる教材
4. リスニングで登場した英文を使用し、3つのステップを用いたアウトプット活動
5. DVD に登場する大学に関する興味あるリーディングの活動と語彙学習

　実際に話されている英語のリスニング訓練においては、「authentic な多くのノイズ入りの教材」に挑戦する必要があります。この場合のノイズとは、周りの騒音だけではなく、発音や文法のみだれ、言い間違い、声の強弱、異文化に由来する価値観の違い、認識のずれなど、コミュニケーションを妨げるものすべてを言います。ノイズのないリスニング教材をいくら聞いても、実践で役に立つリスニング力は養成されません。本教材は、英国や合衆国の現地で、実際にインタビューをしたり、自己紹介をお願いしたりして制作した、まさに authentic な DVD 教材です。この DVD を使用して、ノイズにも対応できるリスニング力養成を目指します。

　しかしながら、ただ漠然と authentic な教材を聞いても実践的なリスニング力は養成されません。聞き取れなかった部分を「トップダウン処理」と呼ばれる方法で埋めていくような練習が必要です。そのため本書では、Step 1、Step 2、Step3 を用意し、トップダウンの処理方法を意識して効果的に学べるようなタスクを用意しています。

　聞き取れるようになった英文の一部は、スピーキングやライティングにおいて積極的に活用し、アウトプットの力も伸ばします。リスニングの部分の学習を最大限活用し、Step 1、Step 2、Step3 と、だんだん難しいタスクに挑戦します。そうすることで、自信をもって話したり書いたりできるようになります。

　リーディングに関しては、DVD に登場する大学に関する興味深い内容の英文を読みます。大学の成り立ちや特徴、さらに学生生活など、DVD の内容と合わせて楽しめるようになっています。また、ここでも「トップダウン処理」の訓練になるよう、工夫されたリーディングのタスクが用意されています。また同時に、語彙学習を行い、アウトプットにも生かせるようになっています。

　本書を利用して、大学生のみなさんが、実践的な、しかも4技能のバランスの取れた英語力を身につけることを期待いたします。本書は4年前に構想されて、年月を重ねて完成にいたりました。本書の出版や編集において数々のアドバイスをいただき、本書の完成にご尽力いただきました英宝社社長佐々木元氏と編集長下村幸一氏に、こころよりお礼申し上げます。

2020 年晩秋

著者代表
小笠原　真司

Contents

Unit 1
Self-introduction (1):
The University of Edinburgh, University Student

1 Comprehension Step 1　DVD 1

エジンバラ大学の図書館前で、ちょっと恥ずかしがり屋の大学生に自己紹介をお願いしました。
DVD を見て、以下の質問に日本語で答えましょう。

1. Jane さんは文系の学生ですか、それとも理系の学生ですか。

   _____

2. 勉強以外に、彼女は何が楽しいと言っていますか。

   _____

2 Key Words Step 2

DVD に出てきた重要語の確認をしましょう。選択欄から最も適切な日本語を選びましょう。また、
CD を用いて発音の練習もしましょう。

1. astrophysics _____
2. humanities _____
3. further _____
4. load _____

人文科学	仕事量、勉強量	さらに（遠く）	天体物理学

3 Comprehension Step 2　DVD 1

重要語の確認ができたので、1回目よりは聞き取りやすくなっていると思います。それでは、もう
一度 DVD を見て、もう少し細かな内容まで聞き取り、以下の質問に日本語で答えましょう。

1. 彼女はこのキャンパスにはあまり来ないようです。どうしてでしょうか。

   _____

2. 人文関係の学部がある場所の名前は、何ですか。

   _____

3. 彼女はエジンバラ大学の学生であることが自慢のようです。それを表している英文を聞き取っ
   て書きましょう。

   It's _____

4 Dictation Step 3

DVD 1

CD を聞いて、下線部 (1) ～ (5) の部分に英語を書き入れて、スクリプトを完成しましょう。スクリプトを完成したら、もう一度 DVD を見てみましょう。

I study Astrophysics at the University of Edinburgh here. My campus is (1)_____

_____ . It's (2)_____

Campus. So, in Edinburgh they have the Humanities Campus here (3)_____

_____ , and then the Science Campus a little bit further away. And I

really enjoy Edinburgh as a city. (4)_____ .

There's loads going on for a student. I have (5)_____

_____ , so that's really fun. "Edinburgh, it's great to meet you."

Let's Write and Speak. ☺

5 Useful Expressions Step 1

DVD の中に出てきた構文を使用した表現です。CD を聞いてリピーティングを行い、暗記するまで練習しましょう。

1. I study economics at the University of Edinburgh.

（私はエジンバラ大学で経済学を勉強しています）

2. The Science Campus is a little bit further away.

（理系学部のキャンパスは、少し離れたところにあります）

6 | Writing and Speaking Step 2

Useful Expressions を利用して、以下の下線に英語を入れて、自分のことを話してみましょう。

1. I study _____ at _____.

2. The _____ is a little bit further away.

7 | Writing and Speaking Step 3

4のスクリプトを参考にして、自分自身のことを話してみましょう。6で作成した英文も利用しましょう。

_____

_____

_____

_____

_____

Let's Read. ☺

8 | Key Words Step 1

Reading Passage に出てくる重要語を確認しましょう。選択欄から最も適切な日本語を選びましょう。また、CD を用いて発音の練習もしましょう。

1. found _____   2. intellectual _____

3. survey _____   4. leading _____

5. fund _____   6. literature _____

7. politics _____   8. head _____

9. Prime Minister _____   10. winner _____

11. notable _____   12. alumni _____

文学	卒業生たち	創立する	注目すべき
主要な	受賞者	資金を提供する	政治（学）
長	調査	総理大臣	知的な

7

次の英文は、エジンバラ大学の概要を説明しています。英文を速読して、エジンバラ大学に関する以下の質問に、日本語で答えましょう。

The University of Edinburgh was **founded** in 1582 and is the sixth-oldest university in the English-speaking world. Located in the city of Edinburgh, the university has five main campuses, many of which form a part of the historic Old Town. The university was known as a key **intellectual** center during the Enlightenment and earned the nickname "Athens of the North."

The University of Edinburgh is one of the top-ranked universities in the world, named 20th best in the world and 6th best in Europe in University ranking **surveys**. It is also a **leading** research university, ranked 4th in the U.K. and 11th overall. It is the third-highest **funded** university in the U.K. after Cambridge and Oxford.

The University has been attended by many world leaders who achieved lasting places in the history of science, **literature**, **politics**, and economics, including 9 **heads** of state (3 **Prime Ministers** of the U.K.), 19 Nobel Prize **winners**, and 2 Pulitzer Prize winners. Among these **notable alumni** were Alexander Graham Bell, Arthur Conan Doyle (of "Sherlock Holmes" fame), Charles Darwin, and Robert Louis Stevenson.

(注) the Enlightenment （主に 18 世紀ヨーロッパの）啓蒙運動。

1. どんな点で6番目に歴史のある大学ですか。

　　_____

2. かつて、どのような愛称で呼ばれていましたか。

　　_____

3. 主要な研究大学としてどのような位置にありますか。

　　_____

4. ケンブリッジ大学やオックスフォード大学に次いで、どのような点で優れていますか。

　　_____

5. 特にどのような4つの分野で歴史に名を残す人を輩出していますか。

　　_____

6. コナン・ドイルやチャールズ・ダーウィンの共通点は何ですか。

　　_____

Unit 2

Self-introduction (2):
The University of Edinburgh, University Student

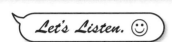 *Let's Listen.* ☺

1 Comprehension Step 1 `DVD 2`

今度はエジンバラ大学のキャンパスで、音楽が大好きな大学生に自己紹介をお願いしてみました。彼女は、2度自己紹介をしてくれます。DVD を見て、以下の質問に日本語で答えましょう。

1. Melissa さんの専攻は何でしょうか。

   _____

2. 彼女はどこの出身ですか。

   _____

2 Key Words Step 2

DVD に出てきた重要語の確認をしましょう。選択欄から最も適切な日本語を選びましょう。また、CD を用いて発音の練習もしましょう。

1. literature _____ 2. focus on _____

3. sociable _____ 4. opportunity _____

5. get involved in _____ 6. experience _____

経験する　文学　　機会　　なごやかな　　～にのめり込む　　重点的にする

3 Comprehension Step 2 `DVD 2`

重要語の確認ができたので、1回目よりは聞き取りやすくなっていると思います。それでは、もう一度 DVD を見て、もう少し細かな内容まで聞き取り、以下の質問に日本語で答えましょう。

1. 彼女は専門の中でも、どのような分野に興味がありますか。

   _____

2. エジンバラの天気の様子は、どのような感じですか。

   _____

3. 彼女は勉強の他にどのようなことに興味がありますか。

   _____

4. エジンバラに来て、どんな経験ができてよいと言っていますか。

_____

4 Dictation Step 3 DVD 2

CD を聞いて、下線部 (1) ～ (7) の部分に英語を書き入れて、スクリプトを完成しましょう。スクリプトを完成したら、もう一度 DVD を見てみましょう。

Self-introduction 1   My name is Melissa. (1)_____

____ and I'm in my second year at the University of Edinburgh. This year we're

gonna (2)_____, so texts written in

English from the 20th and 21st century. I really love living in Edinburgh. It's a

very beautiful city with a lot of history, and it's very sociable as well. It's very easy

to make friends here. But it can (3)_____.

Yeah, and there's lots of opportunities to get involved (4)_____

_____ (and) things like that.

Self-introduction 2   My name is Melissa. I'm in my second year at the

University of Edinburgh. (1)_____, and this year I'm going to be reading lots

of texts from the 20th and 21st century, (5)_____

written in English. Umm, I've really enjoyed my time here so far. Edinburgh is a

very beautiful city, there's lots of history here and it's very nice. (6)_____

経験する
_____, so it's nice to experience (7)_____

_____, and do Scottish dancing and play Scottish music sometimes.

Let's Write and Speak. ☺

5 Useful Expressions Step 1 CD 1-9

DVD の中に出てきた構文を使用した表現です。CD を聞いてリピーティングを行い、暗記するまで練習しましょう。

1. There are lots of opportunities to get involved in sports.

(スポーツに没頭できる機会がたくさんあります)

2. It's nice to experience some cultural activities very often.

(たびたび文化的活動を経験できるのは素晴らしいです)

6 Writing and Speaking Step 2

Useful Expressions を利用して、以下の下線に英語を入れて、自分のことを話してみましょう。

1. There are lots of opportunities to _____.

2. It's nice to _____ very often.

7 Writing and Speaking Step 3

4のスクリプトを参考にして、自分自身のことを話してみましょう。6で作成した英文も利用しましょう。

_____

_____

_____

_____

_____

Let's Read. ☺

8 Key Words Step 1

Reading Passage に出てくる重要語を確認しましょう。選択欄から最も適切な日本語を選びましょう。また、CD を用いて発音の練習もしましょう。

1. initially _____
2. expand _____
3. grant _____
4. status _____
5. full-fledged _____
6. groundbreaking _____
7. designation _____
8. previous _____
9. the Pope _____
10. embrace _____
11. officially _____
12. populous _____

授与する	革新的な	以前の	ローマ教皇
指定	当初	人口の多い	公式に
本格的な	広げる	地位	容認

11

次の英文は、エジンバラ大学の歴史を説明しています。英文を速読して、エジンバラ大学に関する以下の質問に、日本語で答えましょう。

The University of Edinburgh was established by the Edinburgh Town Council, operating **initially** as a college of law. The Town Council and Ministers of the City worked to **expand** the mission of the university until a Royal Charter from King James VI of Scotland **granted** it **status** as a **full-fledged** college on April 14, 1582. This was a **groundbreaking designation** in the history of Scotland, where all **previous** charters had been granted by **the Pope**, and it reflected Scotland's recent **embrace** of the Presbyterian faith. **Officially** opening its doors to students in October 1583, it became the fourth university in Scotland at a time when wealthier and more **populous** England had only two. Its name was officially changed to King James's college in 1617.

(注) Town Council　英国の町議会　　　Minister　聖職者、牧師
Royal Charter　　英国で国王が法人格を与える勅許のこと。2001年時点で勅許を受けている組織は約750あり、その中には、市、大学、研究機関などが含まれる。
Presbyterian faith　　キリスト教の長老派

1. 当初はどのような分野に特化した大学でしたか。

　　_____

2. 1582年4月に、エジンバラ大学はどうなりましたか。

　　_____

3. 2. のことが、スコットランドの歴史上、groundbreaking designation だった理由は何ですか。

　　_____

4. opening its doors to students とはどのような意味ですか。

　　_____

5. エジンバラ大学がスコットランドで4番目の大学になった当時、イングランドはどのような様子でしたか。

　　_____

Self-introduction (3):
The University of Edinburgh, University Student

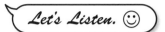 Let's Listen. ☺

1 Comprehension Step 1   DVD 3

今回はエジンバラ大学のキャンパスで、二人の大学生に自己紹介をお願いしてみました。二人の自己紹介を聞いてみましょう。DVD を見て、以下の質問に日本語で答えましょう。

1. Luther 君は、何を専攻していますか。

_____

2. Emily さんは、何を専攻していますか。

_____

2 Key Words Step 2   CD 1-12

DVD に出てきた重要語の確認をしましょう。選択欄から最も適切な日本語を選びましょう。また、CD を用いて発音の練習もしましょう。

1. day-to-day _____ 2. lecture _____

3. tutorial _____ 4. stuff _____

5. Master's Degree _____ 6. look forward to _____

個別指導	楽しみにする	修士号	日常的な	講義	もの、こと

3 Comprehension Step 2   DVD 3

重要語の確認ができたので、1回目よりは聞き取りやすくなっていると思います。それでは、もう一度 DVD を見て、もう少し細かな内容まで聞き取り、以下の質問に日本語で答えましょう。

1. Luther（男子学生）は、起床後どこで勉強しますか。

_____

2. 彼は勉強が終われば何をしますか。

_____

3. 彼は、2 の他に何をしますか。

_____

4. Emily（女子学生）は、専攻の勉強をどのくらいしていますか。

_____

5. 彼女は、最後にどんなことを楽しみにしていると言っていますか。

_____

4 Dictation Step 3 〔DVD 3〕 〔CD 1-13〕

CD を聞いて、下線部 (1) 〜 (7) の部分に英語を書き入れて、スクリプトを完成しましょう。スクリプトを完成したら、もう一度 DVD を見てみましょう。

Self-introduction 1 My name is Luther and I'm a French student at the University of Edinburgh. (1)_____. And on a day-to-day basis, I wake up, I (2)_____, and then I go to lectures and tutorials. And then I finish around 6, and then there's a lot of different activities which I can do here at the university, so I can go to (3)_____ _____, or I can go to (4)_____ about stuff I like. So, yeah, there's lots to do.

Self-introduction 2 Hi, I'm Emily. I'm (5)_____ _____ here at the University of Edinburgh. I'm really excited for this program. I'm hoping that I can learn a lot about Management, the world of Business, and just to discover (6)_____ in Management. Uhh, the school seems great. I'm really excited to be here, I just got here, and I'm really looking forward to (7)_____.

Let's Write and Speak. ☺

5 Useful Expressions Step 1

DVD の中に出てきた構文を使用した表現です。CD を聞いてリピーティングを行い、暗記するまで練習しましょう。

1. There are a lot of different activities which I can do at the university.
   （大学では、できる様々な活動があります）
2. I'm hoping that I can learn a lot about the world of Business.
   （ビジネスの世界について多くのことを学べればと思います）

6 Writing and Speaking Step 2

Useful Expressions を利用して、以下の下線に英語を入れて、自分のことを話してみましょう。

1. There are a lot of _____.

2. I'm hoping that I can _____.

7 Writing and Speaking Step 3

4のスクリプトを参考にして、自分自身のことを話してみましょう。6で作成した英文も利用しましょう。

_____

_____

_____

_____

_____

Let's Read. ☺

8 Key Words Step 1

Reading Passage に出てくる重要語を確認しましょう。選択欄から最も適切な日本語を選びましょう。また、CD を用いて発音の練習もしましょう。

1. rhetoric _____
2. appointment _____
3. architect _____
4. tailor-made _____
5. anatomy _____
6. discipline _____
7. surgery _____
8. deliver _____
9. dissection _____
10. macabre _____
11. murder _____
12. execute _____

届ける、送る	解剖学	建築家	注文仕立ての
殺人事件	任命	学科	解剖
ぞっとするような	修辞学	処刑する	手術

次の英文は、エジンバラ大学の歴史を説明しています。英文を速読して、エジンバラ大学に関する以下の質問に、日本語で答えましょう。

King George III named Reverend Hugh Blair as the first Regius Professor of **Rhetoric** and Belle Lettres in 1762. With this **appointment**, literature was formally established as a subject at the university and Edinburgh became the oldest seat of literary education in Britain. Prior to the Napoleonic Wars in the early 19th century, the campus of the University was a collection of unrelated buildings without a clear design, but at the initiative of Robert Adam, the **architect** William Henry Playfair designed the first **tailor-made** building for the university. This was the Old College, now Edinburgh Law School, located on South Bridge.

It started life as a center for the teaching of **anatomy** and what was at the time a relatively new **discipline**, the science of **surgery**. The Old College building was connected to the basement of a nearby house by an underground tunnel known as the anatomy tunnel corridor. Through this tunnel, bodies were **delivered** for **dissection** to the university's anatomy lecture theater. This tunnel is linked to one of the more **macabre** chapters in Edinburgh history. The Burke and Hare **murders**, a series of 16 murders occurred in Edinburgh for about ten months in 1828. The murderers committed the murders with the express purpose of selling the bodies to the Anatomy College. Ironically, once the killers were tried and Burke, the leader, was **executed**, it was his body that was delivered to the college and dissected.

（注）Regius Professor　欽定講座担当教授　　　Belle Lettres　純文学

1. Reverend Hugh Blair が Regius Professor になり、どんな変化が起こりましたか。

_____

2. Robert Adam は、大学のためにどのようなことをしましたか。

_____

3. Old College では、当初どのような学問が教えられていましたか。

_____

4. Old College の建物は、構造上どのような特徴がありましたか。

_____

5. 下から2行目に Ironically（皮肉にも）とありますが、どのようなことが Ironically なのかを説明しなさい。

_____

Unit 4

Self-introduction (4):
The University of Edinburgh, University Student

 *Let's Listen.* ☺

1 Comprehension Step 1　　　　DVD 4

最後に、エジンバラ大学のキャンパスで、はきはきした留学生に会いました。一番長くしゃべってくれました。彼女の自己紹介を聞いてみましょう。DVD を見て、以下の質問に日本語で答えましょう。

1. Lucy さんは、どこの国の出身でしょうか。

2. 彼女の母語は、何語でしょうか。

2 Key Words Step 2　　　　

DVD に出てきた重要語の確認をしましょう。選択欄から最も適切な日本語を選びましょう。また、CD を用いて発音の練習もしましょう。

1. originally　＿＿＿＿＿＿＿　　2. ecology　＿＿＿＿＿＿＿

3. soil　＿＿＿＿＿＿＿　　4. biology　＿＿＿＿＿＿＿

5. mother tongue　＿＿＿＿＿＿＿　　6. accent　＿＿＿＿＿＿＿

7. environment　＿＿＿＿＿＿＿　　8. enrich　＿＿＿＿＿＿＿

向上させる	母語	もとは	生物学
土壌	生態系	なまり	環境、状況

3 Comprehension Step 2　　　　DVD 4

重要語の確認ができたので、1回目よりは聞き取りやすくなっていると思います。それでは、もう一度 DVD を見て、もう少し細かな内容まで聞き取り、以下の質問に日本語で答えましょう。

1. Lucy さんは、Ecology をどんなことを勉強する学問だと定義していますか。

2. 彼女はどうして、You can hear by my accent. と言ったのでしょうか。

3. 彼女は、今どんな環境で勉強していると言っていますか。

_____

4. 彼女は、大学は学問をするだけでなく、どんな場所だと言っていますか。

_____

4 Dictation Step 3

CD を聞いて、下線部 (1) ～ (6) の部分に英語を書き入れて、スクリプトを完成しましょう。スクリプトを完成したら、もう一度 DVD を見てみましょう。

So my name is Lucy Bisteau. I'm originally from Brussels (1)_____

_____. So I'm European. And I'm studying Ecological and Environmental

Sciences with Management. So it's Ecology - is (2)_____

_____, so Biology before the nature. I've been here studying in the University

of Edinburgh for three years now. Uh, I'm going to my third year and I'm really

enjoying being here. Umm, (3)_____, normally I

speak French. You can hear by my accent. So I've been studying in an environment

(4)_____.

And I found it really enriching, very...uh, I learned a lot (5)_____

_____ from everywhere, from Japan, from Asia, from America, from Europe.

Umm. And I think that the University is not the only way to learn, but (6)_____

_____. Um, yeah. I hope everything is

good in Japan. Nice to meet you. And, yeah, thank you.

> *Let's Write and Speak.* ☺

5 Useful Expressions Step 1

DVD の中に出てきた構文を使用した表現です。CD を聞いてリピーティングを行い、暗記するまで練習しましょう。

1. I've been studying at the University of Edinburgh for three years now.

(エジンバラ大学で 3 年間学んでいます)

2. I think that the University is not the only way to learn, but it's also the place to make friends. (大学は学ぶだけではなく、友達を作る場所だと思います)

6 Writing and Speaking Step 2

Useful Expressions を利用して、以下の下線に英語を入れて、自分のことを話してみましょう。

1. I've been _____.

2. I think that the University is not the only way to _____

   _____.

7 Writing and Speaking Step 3

4のスクリプトを参考にして、自分自身のことを話してみましょう。6で作成した英文も利用しましょう。

_____

_____

_____

_____

_____

Let's Read. ☺

8 Key Words Step 1

CD 1-20

Reading Passage に出てくる重要語を確認しましょう。選択欄から最も適切な日本語を選びましょう。また、CD を用いて発音の練習もしましょう。

1. reputation _____
2. acclaim _____
3. distinction _____
4. commence _____
5. endeavor _____
6. certify _____
7. equality _____
8. legislation _____
9. honor _____
10. plaque _____
11. testament _____
12. persecution _____

平等	証明	努力、試み	迫害
開始する	栄誉を授ける	免許状を与える	評判
称賛する	特色	銘板	法律、法令

次の英文は、エジンバラ大学の歴史を説明しています。英文を速読して、エジンバラ大学に関する以下の質問に、日本語で答えましょう。

The medical school at the University of Edinburgh enjoyed a **reputation** as the best medical school in the English-speaking world during the 18th century, and is still **acclaimed** worldwide. One of its proudest **distinctions** is having opened its doors to the first group of female students enrolled at any British university. Known as the Edinburgh Seven and led by Sophia Jex-Blake, they **commenced** their academic **endeavors** in 1869. Despite being ultimately unsuccessful in their efforts to complete the full course and be **certified** as doctors, they are now seen as pioneers in the drive for women's rights. Their heroic struggle dramatically increased awareness of the need for women's **equality**, and played a key role in winning passage of **legislation** to ensure women the right to study at university in 1877. The first female graduated from the medical school in 1894, and the Edinburgh Seven are now **honored** with a memorial **plaque** at the University of Edinburgh.

Championing the right of women was not the only time the university played a part in helping a disadvantaged group secure their rights to an education. During World War II, the Polish School of Medicine was opened as a "wartime **testament** to the spirit of enlightenment" and provided members of the Polish army fighting **persecution** from both the Nazis and the Soviet Union with the opportunity to study medicine. The classes for these soldiers were conducted in Polish and by the time the school closed in 1949, 336 students had attended classes, 227 graduated with a Bachelor of Medicine and Bachelor of Surgery, and 19 doctors obtained a doctorate or MD.

1. エジンバラ大学医学部は、18 世紀にはどのように言われていましたか。

   _____

2. エジンバラ大学の医学部が自慢（誇り）にしていることの一つは、何ですか。

   _____

3. 1877 年に、どのような変化が起こりましたか。

   _____

4. エジンバラ大学の医学部は、第二次世界大戦中にどのようなことをしましたか。

   _____

5. 第二次世界大戦の終了後、4 のおかげでどのような結果を生み出しましたか。

   _____

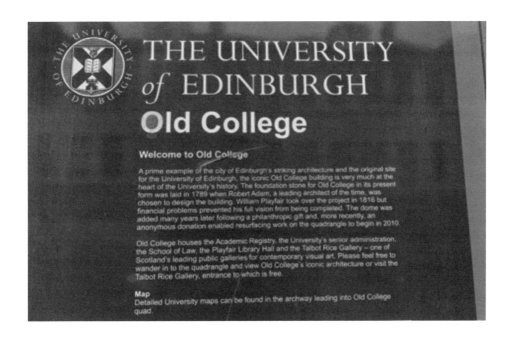

The University of Edinburgh, Old College (Law School)

The University of Edinburgh, Old College (Law School)

Unit 5

Introduction of the former students:
St.Michael's School in Dumfries (Scotland) ,Head Teacher

Let's Listen. ☺

1 Comprehension Step 1 | DVD 5

よく知られたタイタニック号に関連するお話です。タイタニック号は、1912年、北大西洋上で氷山に衝突して沈没し、およそ1500人が亡くなりました。この DVD のダンフリースの町も、タイタニック号と関係がありそうです。DVD を見て、以下の質問に日本語で答えましょう。

1. お話の中で校長先生は、緊張して 1912 年を言い間違えています。何年と言っているでしょうか。

_____

2. John (Jock) Law Hume と Tom Mullin は、どこで会ったと言っていますか。

_____

2 Key Words Step 2

DVD に出てきた重要語の確認をしましょう。選択欄から最も適切な日本語を選びましょう。また、CD を用いて発音の練習もしましょう。

1. former pupil _____   2. go down _____

3. steward _____   4. contact _____

5. fate _____   6. end up _____

7. pure _____   8. offer _____

連絡先	卒業生	単なる	終える
運命	客室係	提案する	沈没する

3 Comprehension Step 2 | DVD 5

重要語の確認ができたので、1回目よりは聞き取りやすくなっていると思います。それでは、もう一度 DVD を見て、もう少し細かな内容まで聞き取り、以下の質問に日本語で答えましょう。

1. タイタニック号に乗船したときの John と Tom のそれぞれの職業は何でしたか。

_____

2. ホワイト・スター・ライン社とタイタニック号の関係について説明しましょう。

_____

3. Tom が John に再会しなければ、どうなっていたと言っていますか。

_____

4 Dictation Step 3

CD を聞いて、下線部 (1) ～ (6) の部分に英語を書き入れて、スクリプトを完成しましょう。スクリプトを完成したら、もう一度 DVD を見てみましょう。

This is a (1)_____ at St Michael's Primary School as it reminds us of two of our former pupils who sadly lost their lives at the *Titanic* (2)_____. And John Law Hume, obviously, (3)_____ for having continued to play as the ship was going down. And we also have Tom Mullin (4)_____ _____ and he, sadly, also lost his life at the Titanic, too.

The story goes that, erm, John Law Hume would come home to visit his family and he was (5)_____ when the young Tom Mullin had come, and he said to him—he was looking for a job—and he said "There's really good money on the ships if you go down to the shipping." So it was actually John Law Hume that had told—given Tom Mullin the contacts to get him to the White Star Liner ships. And it just so happens, (6)_____, that they ended up both on the Titanic (2)_____.

Let's Write and Speak. ☺

5 Useful Expressions Step 1

DVD の中に出てきた構文を使用した表現です。CD を聞いてリピーティングを行い、暗記するまで練習しましょう。

1. The story goes that he was planning to come home to visit his family.
   (話しでは、彼は家族に会いに帰るつもりだったということらしい)
2. It's very interesting to note that their meeting in the pub was pure fate.
   (興味深いことに、彼らのパブでの出会いはまったくの運命だった)

6 Writing and Speaking Step 2

Useful Expressions を利用して、以下の下線に英語を入れて、自分が関心のあることを話してみましょう。

1. The story goes that _____

   _____.

2. It's very interesting to note that _____

   _____.

7 Writing and Speaking Step 3

自分が関心のあることについて話してみましょう。6で作成した英文も、利用しましょう。

_____

_____

_____

_____

_____

_____

 *Let's Read.* ☺

8 Key Words Step 1

Reading Passage に出てくる重要語を確認しましょう。選択欄から最も適切な日本語を選びましょう。また、CD を用いて発音の練習もしましょう。

1. liner _____
2. mill _____
3. promotion _____
4. disaster _____
5. cable-lying _____
6. cast off _____
7. wharf _____
8. body _____
9. vessel _____
10. granite _____
11. on duty _____
12. abandon _____
13. head off _____
14. pregnant _____

工場	出発する	惨劇・悲劇	死体
船	昇進	勤務中	ケーブル敷設の
食い止める	波止場	御影石	旅客船
放棄する	妊娠した		

次の英文は、St. Michael's School 出身で、タイタニック号で亡くなった二人の若者について紹介しています。英文を速読して、以下の質問に、日本語で答えましょう。

Two young Dumfries men, John (Jock) Law Hume and Tom Mullin, died when the *Titanic* hit an iceberg and sank in the Atlantic Ocean on April 15, 1912. Jock was a talented violinist who played with the ship's band. He had been playing the violin on many passenger liners since he was fourteen. At the age of twenty-one, he had had the chance to play on the greatest ocean **liner** ever built. It was his bad luck that it was the *Titanic*. On the other hand, Tom used to be a **mill** worker, but he was advised by Jock to be a steward and became a third-class steward on passenger ships. He got on very well in his new career and **promotion** was likely. Following Jock's advice was to cost Tom his life. He was twenty when he boarded on the *Titanic*.

After the **disaster**, on April 17, the **cable-lying** ship *Mackey-Bennett* **cast off** from the **wharf** in Halifax Nova Scotia in Canada. The ship's mission was to recover the dead and bring the **bodies** back to Halifax, the nearest port to where the *Titanic* went under. Luckily, Jock's and Tom's bodies were recovered and carried to Halifax (Tom's body was recovered by other searching **vessels**, the *Montmagny* and the *Algerine*). The two young men are buried in the same cemetery, Fairview Lawn Cemetery in Halifax. In Dumfries, their memorial, a **granite** obelisk, was unveiled in 1913, in Dock Park.

Although not **on duty** when the order came to **abandon** ship, Jock and his fellow bandsmen went on deck and continued to play until the ship went down. The eight brave musicians met their deaths while performing an act which was of the greatest service in assisting to maintain discipline and **head off** panic. Survivors reported that the last piece of music the band played was the hymn 'Nearer, My God, To Thee,'. He was only twenty-one and left behind his **pregnant** fiancée, Mary Costin in Dumfries. His daughter was named Johnann Law Hume in his memory. In *And the Band Played On*, Jock's grandson Christopher Ward has written a moving account of his grandfather, Jock's brief but brave life.

(注) Halifax　カナダ、ノヴァ・スコシア州にある、大西洋に面した港湾都市。ノヴァ・スコシア州の州都。

1. Jock (John) と Tom が死亡した理由は何ですか。

　_____

2. Tom はどうしてタイタニック号に乗ることになりましたか。

　_____

3. 二人のお墓は、どうしてカナダにあるのですか。

　_____

4.Jock (John) と Tom の記念碑は、どこにありますか。

_____

5. なぜ、Jock (John) たち楽団員は演奏を続けたのですか。

_____

6. 生存者たちは楽団に関して、どのようなことを語っていますか。

_____

7. *And the Band Played On* を出版した人は、どのような人ですか。

_____

The marble plaque commemorating Jock and Tom(St.Michael's school)

The simple granite head stone in Fairview Lawn Cemetery, Halifax, marking Jock's grave, No,193.

Picture of the obelisk in Dock Park, Dumfries in memory of Jock and his school friend Tom Mullin, who died with him on the Titanic.

The Eight Musicians of the Titanic. Jock is pictured bottom right.

Unit 6

Interview (1): California State University Monterey Bay, International Student

Let's Listen. ☺

1 Comprehension Step 1   DVD 7

カリフォルニア州立大学モントレーベイ校の留学生にインタビューをしました。DVD を見て、以下の質問に日本語で答えましょう。

1. この学生は何年生ですか。

_____

2. 彼女はいくつ仕事をしていると言っていますか。

_____

2 Key Words Step 2   CD 1-27

DVD に出てきた重要語の確認をしましょう。選択欄から最も適切な日本語を選びましょう。また、CD を用いて発音の練習もしましょう。

1. senior   _____
2. Women's Studies   _____
3. in private   _____
4. domestic   _____
5. orientation   _____
6. deliver   _____

女性学	国内の	伝える	最上級生	個人的に	説明会

3 Comprehension Step 2   DVD 7

重要語の確認ができたので、1回目よりは聞き取りやすくなっていると思います。それでは、もう一度 DVD を見て、もう少し細かな内容まで聞き取り、以下の質問に日本語で答えましょう。

1. 彼女はいつ卒業予定だと言っていますか。

_____

2. 彼女は、主にどんなことに焦点を当てた学問を学んでいますか。

_____

3. 6月に何があると言っていますか。

_____

CD を聞いて、下線部 (1) 〜 (5) の部分に英語を書き入れて、スクリプトを完成しましょう。スクリプトを完成したら、もう一度 DVD を見てみましょう。

Interviewer: So, what year are you?

Student: I am a (1)_____, so I will (2) _____

_____.

Interviewer: Okay. And what is your major?

Student: I'm doing Human Communication

and (3) _____

_____.

Interviewer: Oh, wow. Okay, so, what kinds of things do you study?

Student: Um, so Communication is really wide, so we study like how, basically

like how we communicate and how to be an effective communicator,

and we also study History, Literature, and pretty much everything, so

the main focus is to be effective communicator in order to (4) _____

_____ and at

the work place, and (5) _____…like…life and…

so it's everywhere, communication is everywhere, so…

Interviewer: Oh.

Student: we study that…how to communicate better.

Interviewer: Wow, great. Sounds pretty interesting.

Let's Write and Speak. ☺

DVD の中に出てきた構文を使用した表現です。CD を聞いてリピーティングを行い、暗記するまで練習しましょう。

1. I'm doing Human Communication with a concentration in Women's Studies.
   （私は人間コミュニケーション、その中でも特に女性学を勉強しています）
2. I deliver all the information that they have to know.
   （私は彼らが知らなければいけない全ての情報を伝えています）

6 Writing and Speaking Step 2

Useful Expressions を利用して、以下の下線に英語を入れて、自分のことを話してみましょう。

1. I'm doing _____.

2. I deliver _____.

7 Writing and Speaking Step 3

4のスクリプトを参考にして、自分自身のことを話してみましょう。6で作成した英文も利用しましょう。

_____

_____

_____

_____

_____

Let's Read. ☺

8 Key Words Step 1

CD 1-30

Reading Passage に出てくる重要語を確認しましょう。選択欄から最も適切な日本語を選びましょう。また、CD を用いて発音の練習もしましょう。

1. pursue	_____	2. residential	_____
3. idyllic	_____	4. ethnic	_____
5. enroll	_____	6. encounter	_____
7. behest	_____	8. occupy	_____
9. commit	_____	10. legacy	_____
11. low-income	_____	12. measure	_____

民族的	低所得者	占有する	宿泊施設のある
遺産	追求する	要請	入学させる
尺度	関わる	のどかな	出会う

カリフォルニア州立大学モントレーベイ校について説明しています。英文を速読して、以下の質問に日本語で答えましょう。

Students at California State University Monterey Bay can **pursue** their studies in a pleasant **residential** campus located just one mile from the **idyllic** Monterey Bay. Over 7,500 students from diverse religious and **ethnic** backgrounds are currently **enrolled** at CSUMB, creating an environment where they can expand their horizons by **encountering** a wide range of viewpoints and life experiences. The university offers a selection of 25 undergraduate and seven graduate majors and provides individual guidance for each student.

CSUMB was established at the **behest** of community leaders and educators in 1994 on land formerly **occupied** by the Fort Ord United States Army Post. The university is **committed** to honoring the **legacy** of Fort Ord and working to contribute to the Monterey County Economy.

While CSUMB welcomes students from all over the state of California, 38 percent of our undergraduates are from Monterey, San Benito, and Santa Cruz counties. An important part of our mission at CSUMB is extending the benefits of education to **low-income** residents of the Monterey Bay region who were previously unable to afford it. An important tool to achieve this is financial aid, which 72 percent of our student body relies on, and it is a **measure** of the success of our mission that 53 percent of our students are among the first in their generation to attend college. In addition, 52 percent of our students live on campus, giving the campus a sense of community.

1. モントレーベイからキャンパスまでどれくらい離れていますか。

_____

2. どんな学生が入学していると言っていますか。

_____

3. この大学の重要なミッションは何だと言っていますか。

_____

4. どれくらいの学生がキャンパス内に住んでいると言っていますか。

_____

Unit 7

Interview (2): California State University Monterey Bay, International Student

 *Let's Listen.* ☺

1 Comprehension Step 1 `DVD 9`

引き続き、カリフォルニア州立大学モントレーベイ校の留学生へのインタビューです。DVD を見て、以下の質問に日本語で答えましょう。

1. インタビュアーは最初にどのような質問をしていますか。

　　_____

2. 彼女は、何年間この大学にいると言っていますか。

　　_____

2 Key Words Step 2 `CD 1-32`

DVD に出てきた重要語の確認をしましょう。選択欄から最も適切な日本語を選びましょう。また、CD を用いて発音の練習もしましょう。

1. develop _____　　2. challenge _____

3. language barrier _____　　4. in terms of _____

5. embarrassed _____　　6. humiliated _____

> 言葉の壁　　～に関して　　恥ずかしい思いをして　　当惑して　　困難な課題　　発展させる

3 Comprehension Step 2 `DVD 9`

重要語の確認ができたので、1回目よりは聞き取りやすくなっていると思います。それでは、もう一度 DVD を見て、もう少し細かな内容まで聞き取り、以下の質問に日本語で答えましょう。

1. なぜ、彼女は留学生の手助けができると感じているのでしょうか。

　　_____

2. なぜ、アジア諸国からの留学生への情報伝達に困難さを感じていますか。

　　_____

3. ホームシックになった理由としてどのようなことを言っていますか。

　　_____

CD を聞いて、下線部 (1) 〜 (6) の部分に英語を書き入れて、スクリプトを完成しましょう。スクリプトを完成したら、もう一度 DVD を見てみましょう。

Interviewer: And how about any challenges in this job?

Student: Challenges...Well, (1)_____ for me. So, I, I've been (2)_____, so I can speak English well, but still I have some difficulty in terms of delivering information, and plus, (3)_____ _____, so, especially students from Asia compare to other students from Europe or other places, their English level is (4)_____ theirs. So, even though we try to deliver all the information, they don't understand sometimes. And even though they don't understand, they pretend they understand, because sometimes they feel um, (5)_____ if they don't understand in it something, so that's, that's one thing really hard for me to know (6)_____ they understand all the information we gave them, and just to, yeah communicate.

Interviewer:Uh-huh.

Let's Write and Speak. ☺

DVD の中に出てきた構文を使用した表現です。CD を聞いてリピーティングを行い、暗記するまで練習しましょう。

1. I'm able to develop and make a better program for students.
   　　　　(私は、学生のためにこのプログラムをより良くし、発展させることができる)

2. I don't feel that anymore. 　　　　　　　　(私は、今はそのように思わなくなった)

6 Writing and Speaking Step 2

Useful Expressions を利用して、以下の下線に英語を入れて、自分のことを話してみましょう。

1. I'm able to _____.

2. I don't feel _____.

7 Writing and Speaking Step 3

4のスクリプトを参考にして、自分自身のことを話してみましょう。6で作成した英文も利用しましょう。

_____

_____

_____

_____

_____

Let's Read. ☺

8 Key Words Step 1

CD
1-35

Reading Passage に出てくる重要語を確認しましょう。選択欄から最も適切な日本語を選びましょう。また、CD を用いて発音の練習もしましょう。

1. set ~ apart _____   2. decommission _____

3. trace back _____   4. peaking _____

5. noted _____   6. complete _____

7. repurpose _____   8. approve _____

9. go-ahead _____   10. Executive Dean _____

11. property _____   12. inaugurate _____

さかのぼる	発足させる	ゴーサイン	ピーク
際立たせる	廃止する	承認する	土地
学長、総長	別の目的で再利用する	有名な	終える

カリフォルニア州立大学モントレーベイ校について説明をしています。英文を速読して、以下の質問に、日本語で答えましょう。

California State University Monterey Bay (CSUMB) has a unique history which **sets us apart**.

The campus was formerly the site of Fort Ord, a **decommissioned** Army base whose history **traces back** to 1917. Fort Ord was a major site for basic training during the 50s, 60s and 70s, **peaking** during the Vietnam War. Many **noted** personalities such as musician Jimi Hendrix and actor Clint Eastwood performed their basic training here. By the end of Fort Ord's run a total of more than 1.5 million men and women had **completed** their training there.

When Fort Ord was closed in the summer of 1993 by order of Congress, the local community saw an opportunity to **repurpose** the base as a university. A year after that, CSUMB was officially **approved** as the 21st campus in the California State University (CSU) system. The idea was given the **go-ahead** in June 1994. Hank Hendrickson, **Executive Dean** of CSUMB, said, "We became the legal owner of the **property**, and work on the buildings can begin." and he officially **inaugurated** the university.

（注）Jimi Hendrix　アメリカのギタリスト、シンガーソングライター。
　　　Clint Eastwood　アメリカの映画俳優、映画監督。

1. キャンパスの場所にあって廃止されたものは何ですか。

_____

2. 廃止された建物が一番使われていた時期はいつですか。

_____

3. モントレーベイ校は何番目のキャンパスですか。

_____

4. Hank Hendrickson はどのような立場の人ですか。

_____

5. the property とは何を指していますか。

_____

Unit 8

Interview (3):
California State University
Monterey Bay, Staff Member

Let's Listen. ☺

1 Comprehension Step 1 　　　　　　　　　　　　　DVD 11

今度は、CSUMB のスタッフの方にインタビューをしました。彼女はあるプログラムに関係しているようです。DVD を見て、以下の質問に日本語で答えましょう。

1. Amy さんは、このプログラムに関してどのようなポジションについていますか。

　_____

2. このプログラムが、開始したのはいつですか。

　_____

2 Key Words Step 2 　　　　　　　　　　　　　

DVD に出てきた重要語の確認をしましょう。選択欄から最も適切な日本語を選びましょう。また、CD を用いて発音の練習もしましょう。

1. sponsor 　　　_____ 　　2. government 　　_____

3. do a degree 　_____ 　　4. intensive 　　　_____

学位をとる	政府	支援する	短期集中的な

3 Comprehension Step 2 　　　　　　　　　　　　DVD 11

重要語の確認ができたので、1回目よりは聞き取りやすくなっていると思います。それでは、もう一度 DVD を見て、もう少し細かな内容まで聞き取り、以下の質問に日本語で答えましょう。

1. このプログラムを最初に利用したのは、どこの国の学生ですか。

　_____

2. そのプログラムの内容は、どのようなものでしたか。

　_____

3. 3~4 週間のプログラムでは、どのようなことを学ぶことができますか。

　_____

4 Dictation Step 3

CD を聞いて、下線部 (1) 〜 (6) の部分に英語を書き入れて、スクリプトを完成しましょう。スクリプトを完成したら、もう一度 DVD を見てみましょう。

> *Interviewer*: Hi, can you please tell me your name and position at Cal State Monterey Bay?
>
> *Director*: Hi, my name is Amy Lehman and (1)_____ _____ here at CSUMB.
>
> *Interviewer*: Okay, and can I ask you how many visiting university programs you have here at CSUMB?
>
> *Director*: Uh, we have about (2)_____ _____.
>
> *Interviewer*: Wow. And what are some of the different countries students come from?
>
> *Director*: Uh, well, we have students from all over the world. Uh, we have (3)_____countries.
>
> *Interviewer*: And what universities from Japan do you have?
>
> *Director*: Uh, we've had visiting students from Nagasaki, Osaka, Meiji University, Yokohama National University, uh, Oberlin.
>
> *Interviewer*: And what was the first program?
>
> *Director*: Our first program was (4)_____ students who were (5)_____to come and learn English, and (6)_____ here at the university.

Let's Write and Speak. ☺

5 Useful Expressions Step 1

DVD の中に出てきた構文を使用した表現です。CD を聞いてリピーティングを行い、暗記するまで練習しましょう。

1. Can you please tell me your name and position at CSUMB?
   （あなたのお名前と CSUMB でのお仕事を教えてください）

2. Can I ask you how many university exchange programs you have here?
   （ここで提供している交換留学プログラムはいくつあるのか教えてください）

6 Writing and Speaking Step 2

Useful Expressions を利用して、以下の下線に英語を入れて、大学の留学プログラム担当者にインタビューしてみましょう。

1. Can you please tell me your _____ at _____?

2. Can I ask you how many _____ you have here?

7 Writing and Speaking Step 3

4のスクリプトを参考にして、大学関係者になったつもりで、ダイアローグを完成させてみましょう。さらに、6で作成した質問に加えて、独自の質問も加えてみましょう。

Interviewer: Can you please tell me your _____

at _____ ?

( ):_____.

Interviewer: Can I ask you how many _____

_____ you have here?

( ):_____.

Interviewer: _____ ?

( ):_____.

> *Let's Read.* ☺

8 Key Words Step 1

Reading Passage に出てくる重要語を確認しましょう。選択欄から最も適切な日本語を選びましょう。また、CD を用いて発音の練習もしましょう。

1. administrator _____
2. unveil _____
3. enshrine _____
4. philosophy _____
5. aspiration _____
6. dedication _____
7. cutting-edge _____
8. achievement _____
9. panel _____
10. academic _____
11. accreditation _____
12. ethical _____

哲学	委員会	公にする	最先端の
研究者	竣工（式）	倫理の	正式に記されている
成果・業績	管理者	強い願望	認可

カリフォルニア大学モントレーベイ校に関する英文を速読して、以下の質問に日本語で答えましょう。

The opportunity to build a new university attracted many of the finest educators and **administrators** in Monterey Bay to shape it by contributing their talent and ideas. The university **unveiled** its Vision Statement, a document that **enshrines** our fundamental principles and educational **philosophy** and also our aims and **aspirations**. Classes at CSUMB started on August 28, 1995, and while those who were around then can attest that the university was still a "work-in-progress," the **dedication** ceremony was attended by then-president Bill Clinton.

CSUMB developed and expanded in the years that followed, increasing the number of majors available to students, generating more athletic teams, building classroom buildings and residence halls with **cutting-edge** technology, and receiving growing praise for our **achievements**. In particular, our Service Learning program was highlighted in U.S. News, Intel praised our wireless accessibility and the **panel** of **academics** who gave us **accreditation** stressed our **ethical** standards and our socially responsible emphasis on assembling a diverse community of faculty and students.

1. モントレーベイに大学を新設したことで、どのような人が集まってきましたか。

   _____

2. Vision Statement とは、どのようなものですか。

   _____

3. 1995 年当時の大統領は、何をしましたか。

   _____

4. receiving growing praise for our achievements とはどのような意味ですか。

   _____

5. U.S. News は、何をしてくれましたか。

   _____

6. この大学を認可した委員会は、どんな点を評価しましたか。

   _____

Interview (4):
California State University
Monterey Bay, Staff Member

 *Let's Listen.* ☺

1 Comprehension Step 1 　　　　　　　DVD 13

CSUMB のスタッフの方の、後半のインタビューを聞いてみましょう。DVD を見て、以下の質問に日本語で答えましょう。

1. 短期留学プログラムに参加する学生は、テストのスコアが必要ですか。

　_____

2. 短期と比較して、長期の留学プログラムの違いを表す英語を1語指摘しましょう。

　_____

2 Key Words Step 2 　　　　　　　　

DVD に出てきた重要語の確認をしましょう。選択欄から最も適切な日本語を選びましょう。また、CD を用いて発音の練習もしましょう。

1. preparation _____
2. aquarium _____
3. fuzzy _____
4. squirrel _____
5. sea otter _____
6. seal _____

水族館	アザラシ	ラッコ	準備	羽毛で覆われた	リス

3 Comprehension Step 2 　　　　　　　DVD 13

重要語の確認ができたので、1回目よりは聞き取りやすくなっていると思います。それでは、もう一度 DVD を見て、もう少し細かな内容まで聞き取り、以下の質問に日本語で答えましょう。

1. 短期留学プログラムで、特に焦点を当てて教わる内容は何ですか。

　_____

2. 長期留学プログラムの学生が、必要とされているものと必要とされないものは、それぞれ何ですか。

　_____

3. downtown Cannery Row には、何がたくさんありますか。

　_____

CD を聞いて、下線部 (1) ～ (5) の部分に英語を書き入れて、スクリプトを完成しましょう。スクリプトを完成したら、もう一度 DVD を見てみましょう。

> *Interviewer*: And what kinds of things do students study in the longer programs?
>
> *Director*: The longer program is a little more academic.(1)＿＿＿＿＿＿＿＿＿＿＿
> ＿＿＿＿＿＿＿＿＿＿, uh, Academic Oral Speaking and Presentations,
> American Culture and Language Lab and Academic Readiness courses.
>
> *Interviewer*: Oh, wow, great. And, what kinds of activities and trips do students
> make in Monterey and San Francisco?
>
> *Director*: (2)＿＿＿＿＿＿＿＿＿＿＿＿＿＿＿＿＿＿＿＿＿＿＿＿. We have a
> lot to do here in Monterey. Students always visit the famous Monterey
> Bay Aquarium and see all the sea life. Downtown Cannery Row (3)＿＿＿＿
> ＿＿＿＿＿＿＿＿＿＿＿＿＿＿＿＿＿＿＿＿＿. We do bikes to the
> beach, we go to Carmel by the sea. San Francisco we see the Golden
> Gate Bridge, Union Square, um, Pier 39, Twin Peaks, and there's
> always Chinatown and Japan town – lots of shopping there, too.
>
> *Interviewer*: Wow, great, sounds so fun. Um, and I hear there are some special
> animals you can see here in Monterey.
>
> *Director*: Yes, yes, we have lots of nature and wildlife here in Monterey Bay.
> On campus (4)＿＿＿＿＿＿＿＿＿＿＿＿＿＿＿＿＿＿＿＿＿＿＿＿＿
> ＿＿＿＿＿＿＿, and, uh, out in the ocean you'll see lots of really (5)＿＿＿＿
> ＿＿＿＿＿＿＿＿＿＿＿＿＿＿＿＿＿＿＿＿, dolphins, and seals.
>
> *Interviewer*: Great. Thank you so much, Amy.

Let's Write and Speak. ☺

DVD の中に出てきた構文を使用した表現です。CD を聞いてリピーティングを行い、暗記するまで練習しましょう。

1. What kinds of things do students study in the longer programs?

   （長期留学プログラムでは、学生はどんなことを学べますか）

2. What kinds of activities and trips do students make in Monterey?

   （モントレーでは、どのような活動や小旅行ができますか）

6 **Writing and Speaking** Step 2

Useful Expressions を利用して、以下の下線に英語を入れて、大学の留学プログラム担当者にインタビューしてみましょう。

1. What kinds of things do students _____?

2. What kinds of _____?

7 **Writing and Speaking** Step3

4のスクリプトを参考にして、大学関係者になったつもりで、ダイアローグを完成させてみましょう。さらに、6で作成した質問に加えて、独自の質問も加えてみましょう。

Interviewer: What kinds of things do students _____?

(　　　　　): _____.

Interviewer: What kinds of _____?

(　　　　　): _____.

Interviewr: _____?

(　　　　　): _____.

Let's Read. ☺

8 **Key Words** Step1

CD 2-4

Reading Passage に出てくる重要語を確認しましょう。選択欄から最も適切な日本語を選びましょう。また、CD を用いて発音の練習もしましょう。

1. amenity　_____
2. diverse　_____
3. opt　_____
4. engagement　_____
5. stage　_____
6. stimulating　_____
7. showcase　_____
8. surrounding　_____
9. chaplaincy　_____
10. facility　_____
11. numerous　_____
12. intramural　_____

選ぶ	礼拝所	上演する	周囲の
大学内の	売り込む	多様な	多数の
刺激的な	快適にするもの	施設	関与、参加

カリフォルニア大学モントレーベイ校に関する英文を速読して、以下の質問に日本語で答えましょう。

CSUMB offers a rich mix of campus events, organizations, traditions, and **amenities**. Students are encouraged to participate in campus life and are offered a **diverse** set of options to do so. They may **opt** for personal development by taking part in academic, cultural, or religious activities, or they may decide to focus on **engagement** with the larger community through political or social activities. A variety of recreations and sports are also active on campus, and CSUMB **stages** many cultural events at the World Theater including **stimulating** lectures, lively dance, and film events. These events **showcase** the unique blend of cultures in the **surrounding** community.

There are also a range of services available to CSUMB students that promote health, wellness, and safety. Among these services are the Campus Health Center, the Personal Growth & Counseling Center, Campus **Chaplaincy**, and Student Disability Resources. To maintain physical fitness individual students can use our challenge course, gym, and pool **facilities**, and there are **numerous** group activities such as surfing, kayaking, mountain biking, and **intramural** sports. CSUMB takes student safety very seriously and our Student Affairs staff coordinates with campus police to keep our campus safe for all students.

1. モントレーベイ校の学生は、どのような活動に参加して、より大きなコミュニティに関与していきますか。

   _____

2. the World Theater ではどのようなイベントが提供されていますか。

   _____

3. the Campus Health Center, the Personal Growth & Counseling Center などは、学生のどのような目的のためにありますか。

   _____

4. 健康を維持するために、学生はどのような施設を利用できますか。

   _____

5. 大学警察は、何の目的のためにいますか。

   _____

Unit 10

Campus Tour (1): California State University Monterey Bay, International Student

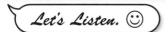 *Let's Listen.* ☺

1 Comprehension Step 1 `DVD 15`

カリフォルニア州立大学モントレーベイ校のキャンパスツアーです。モントレーベイ校の留学生が
キャンパスを案内してくれます。DVD を見て、以下の質問に日本語で答えましょう。

1. Clint Eastwood はこの大学に何を贈りましたか。

   _____

2. Science Building の中はどんな匂いがすると言っていますか。

   _____

2 Key Words Step 2

DVD に出てきた重要語の確認をしましょう。選択欄から最も適切な日本語を選びましょう。また、
CD を用いて発音の練習もしましょう。

1. film director _____ 2. military base _____

3. tear down _____ 4. be obsessed with _____

～に夢中だ	映画監督	軍事基地	取り壊す

3 Comprehension Step 2 `DVD 15`

重要語の確認ができたので、1 回目よりは聞き取りやすくなっていると思います。それでは、もう
一度 DVD を見て、もう少し細かな内容まで聞き取り、以下の質問に日本語で答えましょう。

1. カーメル市とモントレーの位置関係、距離について何と言っていますか。

   _____

2. 案内役の留学生は ground up をどのような意味で使っていますか。

   _____

3. Science Building を設計した人は、何が大好きでしたか。

   _____

4. インタビュアーは、Splash Mountain を聞きまちがえて何と言っていますか。

   _____

CD を聞いて、下線部 (1) ～ (7) の部分に英語を書き入れて、スクリプトを完成しましょう。スクリプトを完成したら、もう一度 DVD を見てみましょう。

Student: So, if you can (1)_____,

Interviewer: Yeah.

Student: So, those are given by a man, Clint, Clint Eastwood. So he is an actor uh, film director, and (2)_____ in Carmel city. So Carmel city is (3)_____ Monterey, so it's from, uh, it's like umm (4)_____ _____ , so he was a Mayor at one time and (5)_____ _____ , because he wanted something shows eternal.

Interviewer: Uh-huh.

Student: or (6)_____,

Interviewer: Right.

Student: So, he gave it to us and…

Interviewer: So, what movie did he direct?

Student: Oh, so (7)_____, uh, " 硫黄島からの手紙 (Io-jima karano tegami)" .

Interviewer: Oh, wow,

Student: Yeah, that's a great movie.

Interviewer: So, he directed that one.

Student: Uh-huh.

Let's Write and Speak. ☺

5 **Useful Expressions** Step 1

DVD の中に出てきた構文を使用した表現です。CD を聞いてリピーティングを行い、暗記するまで練習しましょう。

1. Let me talk a little bit about this science building behind me.
(私の後ろにある科学棟について少しお話ししましょう)

2. He is obsessed with Tokyo Disneyland .　　（彼は、東京ディズニーランドに夢中だ）

6 Writing and Speaking Step 2

Useful Expressions を利用して、以下の下線に英語を入れて、自分のことを話してみましょう。

1. Let me talk a little bit about _____.

2. I am obsessed with _____.

7 Writing and Speaking Step 3

4のスクリプトを参考にして、自分が関心あることを話してみましょう。6で作成した英文も利用しましょう。

_____

_____

_____

_____

_____

Let's Read. ☺

8 Key Words Step 1

CD 2-9

Reading Passage に出てくる重要語を確認しましょう。選択欄から最も適切な日本語を選びましょう。また、CD を用いて発音の練習もしましょう。

1. solid	_____	2. fundamental	_____
3. multi-faceted	_____	4. instill	_____
5. involve	_____	6. pull back	_____
7. grasp	_____	8. marine science	_____
9. applied	_____	10. draw on	_____
11. utilize	_____	12. give someone exposure to	_____

〜を生かす	多角的な	海洋科学	理解する
基礎	しっかりした	教え込む	利用する
触れる機会を与える	〜を取り戻す	関わる、伴う	応用の

47

カリフォルニア州立大学モントレーベイ校のプログラムに関する英文を速読して、以下の質問に日本語で答えましょう。

Students in the Environmental Studies program receive a **solid** training in the **fundamentals** of Environmental Science, which takes a **multi-faceted** approach to the field and includes environmental sciences, social sciences, environmental economics and policy, environmental history, and communication. The program **instills** in students the ability to see the complex issues **involved** in Environmental Science in terms of how they affect the local community, and the region, as well as how to **pull back** and **grasp** the impact on the larger global community. CSUMB also offers an excellent **Marine Science** program whose foundation is a rigorous training in both **applied** learning and research.

The beautiful natural environment of the Monterey Bay area is an ideal setting to pursue this training, which **draws on** lab and field experience to teach students experimental design, data acquisition, analysis, and presentation. Students will learn how to **utilize** these methods, to observe, and to evaluate marine science problems. The program also partners with key agencies in the Monterey Bay area like the Moss Landing Marine Labs, which will **give students exposure to** the skills and know-how of the professionals in the community.

1. 始めにどんな分野のプログラムについて説明されていますか。

　　_____

2. 多角的なアプローチとは、具体的にどんな学問を含みますか。

　　_____

3. 2番目にどんな分野のプログラムについて説明されていますか。

　　_____

4. 2番目の分野のトレーニングにおいて、モントレーベイ校はどうして理想的なのですか。

　　_____

5. 2番目の分野では、具体的にどんな機関と提携していますか。

　　_____

6. 5の機関は、プログラムの学生にどのようなことをしてくれますか。

　　_____

Campus Tour (2): California State University Monterey Bay, International Student

 *Let's Listen.* ☺

1 Comprehension Step 1 　　　　　DVD 17

カリフォルニア州立大学モントレーベイ校のキャンパスツアーの後半です。先ほどの留学生が引き続きキャンパスを案内してくれます。DVD を見て、以下の質問に日本語で答えましょう。

1. 案内役の女性は、日本の大学とアメリカの大学では、学生の違いは何だと言っていますか。

_____

2. North Quad の建物は、どのような人々のためのものですか 。

_____

2 Key Words Step 2 　　　　　CD 2-11

DVD に出てきた重要語の確認をしましょう。選択欄から最も適切な日本語を選びましょう。また、CD を用いて発音の練習もしましょう。

1. dorm _____ 　　2. commute _____

3. depend on _____ 　　4. brand-new _____

真新しい	寮	通う	～しだいである

3 Comprehension Step 2 　　　　　DVD 17

重要語の確認ができたので、1回目よりは聞き取りやすくなっていると思います。それでは、もう一度 DVD を見て、もう少し細かな内容まで聞き取り、以下の質問に日本語で答えましょう。

1. 最初に登場する建物は、どのような人のためのものですか。

_____

2. ルームメイトが1人になるか2人になるかは、何で決まりますか。

_____

3. Promontory とは、どのような建物だと説明していますか。

_____

4 Dictation Step 3

CD を聞いて、下線部 (1) ～ (6) の部分に英語を書き入れて、スクリプトを完成しましょう。スクリプトを完成したら、もう一度 DVD を見てみましょう。

Student:　And, on this side, so those buildings are (1)_____

_____ uh, live there, and…yeah, it's something

uh, special about… uh, America, I think. You know, a lot of uh,

Japanese students who go to Japanese university they don't really live

in a dorm all together. (2)_____ by

themselves or, (3)_____.

Interviewer: Uh-huh.

Student:　So, it's something really different in America.

Interviewer: So, these buildings (4)_____?

Student:　Yeah, there are like five or six, yeah, buildings, and (5)_____

_____.

Interviewer: Oh, wow okay. I guess they have roommates or they live two or three

together.

Student:　Yeah.

Interviewer: Oh, wow.

Student:　Yeah…yeah some, some students have two roommates; some

students have one roommate.

Interviewer: Uh-huh.

Student:　yeah, (6)_____.

Let's Write and Speak. ☺

5 Useful Expressions Step 1

DVD の中に出てきた構文を使用した表現です。CD を聞いてリピーティングを行い、暗記するまで練習しましょう。

1. It's something really different in America.　　（アメリカでは、多少異なります）

2. Some international students live in that studio apartment, or Flat Hope.
   （一部の留学生は、あのワンルームマンション、つまりフラット・ホープに住んでいます）

6 Writing and Speaking Step 2

Useful Expressions を利用して、以下の下線に英語を入れて、自分の知っていることを話してみましょう。

1. _____ is something _____.

2. Some international students live _____.

7 Writing and Speaking Step 3

4のスクリプトを参考にして、大学のことを話してみましょう。6で作成した英文も利用しましょう。

_____

_____

_____

_____

_____

Let's Read. ☺

8 Key Words Step 1

CD
2-14

Reading Passage に出てくる重要語を確認しましょう。選択欄から最も適切な日本語を選びましょう。また、CD を用いて発音の練習もしましょう。

1. expertise _____   2. respective _____

3. distinction _____   4. recipient _____

5. executive _____   6. prestigious _____

7. innovator _____   8. esteem _____

9. entrepreneurship _____   10. foster _____

11. organic _____   12. nonprofit _____

経営幹部	有機栽培の	専門的知識	受賞者
高く評価する	それぞれの	育成する	起業家であること
名声	革新者	非営利の	一流の

51

9 Reading Step 2

カリフォルニア州立大学モントレーベイ校の卒業生は、どのような活躍をしているのでしょうか。
英文を速読して、以下の質問に日本語で答えましょう。

Since the founding of CSUMB in 1994, over 20,000 people have developed the **expertise** and completed the coursework necessary to become graduates in their **respective** fields. Many graduates have gone on to achieve high **distinction** in their chosen fields, including an Academy Award winner of the film industry, a **recipient** of the "teacher of the year" award, an **executive** in the global wine industry, a writer for the **prestigious** New York Times, a researcher at the South Pole, and an **innovator** in online giant LinkedIn.

Many of our graduates have achieved renown in the field of scientific research, including numerous winners of the **esteemed** National Science Foundation fellowship. Other graduates turn to the field of politics, deciding to focus their talents on community organizing. The spirit of initiative and **entrepreneurship fostered** at CSUMB has led many graduates to start their own businesses in areas – ranging from technology firms to restaurants to **organic** farms. Finally, the desire to serve others leads some to work in education and **nonprofit** organizations.

1. become graduates とは、どのような意味でしょうか。

   _____

2. 第一パラグラフでは、どんな分野で活躍している人が紹介されていますか。

   _____

3. 卒業生で、National Science Foundation fellowship を獲得した人はどのくらいいますか。

   _____

4. 多くの卒業生が、様々なビジネスで活躍している背景は何だと言っていますか。

   _____

5. ビジネスで活躍している卒業生に関し、どのような仕事が紹介されていますか。

   _____

Campus Tour (1):
City University of New York, Graduate Student

 Let's Listen. ☺

1 Comprehension Step 1 DVD 19

ニューヨーク市立大学のキャンパスツアーの様子です。大学院生が案内してくれます。DVD を見て、以下の質問に日本語で答えましょう。

1. 最初にこの大学は、何の分野でよく知られていると言っていますか。

   _____

2. 後半でこの大学はどんな点にプライドを持っていると言っていますか。

   _____

2 Key Words Step 2 CD 2-16

DVD に出てきた重要語の確認をしましょう。選択欄から最も適切な日本語を選びましょう。また、CD を用いて発音の練習もしましょう。

1. kindergarten _____
2. linguistic _____
3. undergraduate _____
4. speech pathology _____
5. competitive _____
6. Division _____
7. diverse _____
8. multicultural _____

学部生	部門	言語病理学	幼稚園
多文化的	言語学の	競争のある	多様な

3 Comprehension Step 2 DVD 19

重要語の確認ができたので、1回目よりは聞き取りやすくなっていると思います。それでは、もう一度 DVD を見て、もう少し細かな内容まで聞き取り、以下の質問に日本語で答えましょう。

1. TESOL を学べるのは、どこの学部でしょうか。

   _____

2. 言語病理学のプログラムへ入るのに、とても競争が激しいのはなぜですか。

   _____

3. クラブ活動の数について何と言っていますか。

_____

CD を聞いて、下線部 (1) 〜 (6) の部分に英語を書き入れて、スクリプトを完成しましょう。スクリプトを完成したら、もう一度 DVD を見てみましょう。

    So, this university is very well known for (1)_____

_____. A lot of teachers come out of here. A lot of teachers

once they hear Queen's college they're like "Oh, that's good school!" That happens.

    They're known for their sciences, (2)_____ especially,

very good school, umm, let see, their (3)_____, which is

probably the only the undergraduate programs, that you can do TESOL in. We

have an independent music program building here. The speech pathology program

both (4)_____, is very competitive here, because this one

has one of (5)_____ in New York City, umm,

what else do we have, definitely a celebration of the arts, we have dance studios,

and athletics. I think they're Division 2 which is very very up there, they compete

with St. John's which is nearby, umm, other (6) _____

like Baruch, City College.

Let's Write and Speak. ☺

DVD の中に出てきた構文を使用した表現です。CD を聞いてリピーティングを行い、暗記するまで練習しましょう。

1. This university is very well known for its education program.
            （この大学は、教育プログラムでとてもよく知られている）

2. They pride themselves on the diversity.

（彼らは、多様性に誇りを持っている）

6 | Writing and Speaking Step 2

Useful Expressions を利用して、以下の下線に英語を入れて、自分のことを話してみましょう。

1. My university is very well known for _____.

2. I pride myself on _____.

7 | Writing and Speaking Step 3

4のスクリプトを参考にして、自分自身の大学のことを話してみましょう。6で作成した英文も利用しましょう。

_____

_____

_____

_____

_____

Let's Read. ☺

8 | Key Words Step1

CD
2-19

Reading Passage に出てくる重要語を確認しましょう。選択欄から最も適切な日本語を選びましょう。また、CD を用いて発音の練習もしましょう。

1. unfold _____   2. bear _____

3. inception _____   4. reflect _____

5. conceive _____   6. egalitarian _____

7. fraternity _____   8. opportunity _____

9. upward mobility _____   10. illustrious _____

11. degree-seeking _____   12. matriculate _____

有する、示す	機会	上昇傾向	入学する
平等主義の	友愛	輝かしい	広がる、展開する
発足	～だと考える	学位を目指す	反映する

次の英文は、ニューヨーク市立大学の歴史について説明しています。英文を速読して、以下の質問に日本語で答えましょう。

　　The growth of City University of New York **unfolded** alongside that of the great state whose name it **bears**, and the great country that gave it birth. It is a journey of almost two centuries and began in 1847 with the **inception** of the Free Academy. **Reflecting** the vision of its founder, Townsend Harris, the Free Academy was **conceived** as a place where "the children of the rich and the poor take their seats together." It was this **egalitarian** spirit of **fraternity** between students of all classes that not only propelled the development of CUNY into a great modern university of 25 campuses and half a million students but also spread the **opportunity** for **upward mobility** to sectors of society that had never seen it before.

　　Throughout its **illustrious** history, graduates of CUNY have been recognized for their contributions to science, business, the arts, and a wide range of fields. The university alumni have included 13 Nobel Prize and 26 MacArthur ("Genius") grant winners. At any given time there are over 275,000 **degree-seeking** students as well as 250,000 continuing education and certificate students **matriculating** at CUNY.

(注) continuing education and certificate students　聴講や免許取得のため学んでいる学生

1. この大学は、何の発展とともに歩んできましたか。

　　_____

2. Townsend Harris は、この大学とどんな関係がありますか。

　　_____

3. Townsend Harris のビジョンから、この学校はどのような場所だと考えられていましたか。

　　_____

4. この大学は現在どのような規模に発展していますか。

　　_____

5. この大学の卒業生のすばらしい活躍を示す、具体的事実とは何ですか。

　　_____

6. 250,000 人はどのような学生ですか。

　　_____

Campus Tour (2):
City University of New York, Graduate Student

 Let's Listen. ☺

1 Comprehension Step 1 　　　　DVD 21

ニューヨーク市立大学のキャンパスツアーの様子です。DVD を見て、以下の質問に日本語で答えましょう。

1. この Powdermaker Hall では、文系、理系、芸術系、スポーツ系のうち、どのような系の授業を主に受けることができますか。

_____

2. 期末試験中の図書館の開館時間はどうなりますか。

_____

2 Key Words Step 2

DVD に出てきた重要語の確認をしましょう。選択欄から最も適切な日本語を選びましょう。また、CD を用いて発音の練習もしましょう。

1. accounting　　_____　　2. sociology　　_____

3. secondary education　_____　4. conduit　　_____

5. hawk　　_____　　6. pigeon　　_____

| パイプ役 | 鷹 | 社会学 | 中等教育 | 鳩 | 会計学 |

3 Comprehension Step 2 　　　　DVD 21

重要語の確認ができたので、1回目よりは聞き取りやすくなっていると思います。それでは、もう一度 DVD を見て、もう少し細かな内容まで聞き取り、以下の質問に日本語で答えましょう。

1. Powdermaker Hall は、どのような建物ですか。

_____

2. Powdermaker Hall で学べる学問をいくつかあげてみましょう。

_____

3. 鳩の数を制御するために、どのような対策をしていますか。

_____

CD を聞いて、下線部 (1) ～ (6) の部分に英語を書き入れて、スクリプトを完成しましょう。スクリプトを完成したら、もう一度 DVD を見てみましょう。

Oh yeah, this is the library, from Rosenthal Library, umm, very very big library, students come here to study, or to do work to do the research. During finals week, the library's (1) _____ _____. So, (2)_____. So, the students can come here and study for (3)_____during the final's week, which is nice. And also very stressful too, because of the environment the students find. Umm but a lot of students requested it, so, now they do that for the final's week of school. Umm, very nice campus, also holds a clock tower which (4)_____ _____. We have hawks on the campus, by the way, so, (5)_____ _____. So, we have two red hawks, they're around somewhere I don't think you'll see them as easily, but they're meant to (6)_____ _____. But overall very nice, umm, very nice building and a lot of people... it's very popular with students.

Let's Write and Speak. ☺

DVD の中に出てきた構文を使用した表現です。CD を聞いてリピーティングを行い、暗記するまで練習しましょう。

1. Students can take classes and coursework in this building.
   （学生たちは、この建物で授業やコースワークを受けることが可能です）

2. The two red hawks are flying around somewhere on campus.
   （2 羽の赤いタカがキャンパスのこころあたりを飛んでいます）

6 Writing and Speaking Step 2

Useful Expressions を利用して、以下の下線に英語を入れて、自分の大学のことを話してみましょう。

1. Students can _____ on the campus.

2. _____ are around somewhere _____.

7 Writing and Speaking Step 3

4のスクリプトを参考にして、自分自身の大学のことを話してみましょう。6で作成した英文も利用しましょう。

_____

_____

_____

_____

_____

Let's Read. ☺

8 Key Words Step 1

CD 2-24

Reading Passage に出てくる重要語を確認しましょう。選択欄から最も適切な日本語を選びましょう。また、CD を用いて発音の練習もしましょう。

1. pillar _____
2. curricular _____
3. faculty _____
4. physical _____
5. converge _____
6. intellectual _____
7. discovery _____
8. excellence _____
9. document _____
10. house _____
11. general public _____
12. reference _____

集まる	公文書	参照用	知的な
大学の教員	発見	大衆・一般人	カリキュラム上の
優秀さ	保管する	身体（健康）の	中枢・柱

次の英文は、ニューヨーク市立大学の図書館について説明しています。英文を速読して、以下の質問に日本語で答えましょう。

　　The libraries serve as a **pillar** of the academic programs, teaching and learning at CUNY, enabling all of the wide-ranging **curricular** and research activities of the University's **faculty**, researchers and students. Much of the **physical**, social and intellectual life of CUNY **converges** at the university's libraries, with all the members of the university community working together to drive **intellectual discovery** and academic **excellence**.

　　All faculty and students are permitted to use and borrow materials from any of the University's libraries and may do so whatever college they belong to. Teachers from other CUNY colleges as well as Queens College programs may use the library facilities and materials. Many U.S. government **documents** are also **housed** at the library and are open to the **general public** for **reference**.

（注）Queens College　ニューヨーク市立大学クイーンズ校。ニューヨーク市立大学の中で、ニューヨーク市クイーンズ区にあるカレッジ。

1. この図書館は大学でどんな位置にありますか。

　　_____

2. 大学図書館を研究活動のために利用しているのは、どんな人ですか。

　　_____

3. 大学の図書館にどんなものが集まると述べていますか。

　　_____

4. 教員と学生は何をする許可が与えられていますか。

　　_____

5. 図書館に保管され、一般に公開されているものは何ですか。

　　_____

Unit 14

Campus Tour (3):
City University of New York, Graduate Student

Let's Listen. ☺

1 Comprehension Step 1 　　　DVD 23

ニューヨーク市立大学のキャンパスツアーが続きます。DVD を見て、以下の質問に日本語で答えましょう。

1. 前半のビデオで説明している建物では、どのような勉強ができますか。

　　_____

2. 後半のビデオで、今、この男性は何階にいると言っていますか。

　　_____

2 Key Words Step 2 　　　CD 2-26

DVD に出てきた重要語の確認をしましょう。選択欄から最も適切な日本語を選びましょう。また、CD を用いて発音の練習もしましょう。

1. contemporary art 　_____　　2. ceramics 　_____

3. smelt 　　　　　_____　　4. sculpture 　_____

5. revolve 　　　　_____　　6. discipline 　_____

7. architecture 　　_____　　8. full picture 　_____

精錬する	建築方法	陶器	全体像
回転させる	現代美術	彫刻	学問

3 Comprehension Step 2 　　　DVD 23

重要語の確認ができたので、1回目よりは聞き取りやすくなっていると思います。それでは、もう一度 DVD を見て、もう少し細かな内容まで聞き取り、以下の質問に日本語で答えましょう。

1. この建物で学べることを、具体的にあげてみましょう。

　　_____

2. この建物で学生が困ることは、どんなことですか。

　　_____

3. Back Entrance から入ると何階ですか。

_____

4 Dictation Step 3   DVD 24   CD 2-27

CD を聞いて、下線部 (1) 〜 (6) の部分に英語を書き入れて、スクリプトを完成しましょう。スクリプトを完成したら、もう一度 DVD を見てみましょう。

Well, as you can see (1)_____

_____, um, (2)_____.

So, we have two entrances. This is…I call it the back entrance, but there's no really

back or front entrance. I guess the back I call it. But, if you enter from here, you

gonna (3)_____. Um…, if you enter from other

entrance, you start at floor one. You do start at a lower level, but it's still very

interesting to see how (4)_____. So, for example, you

can't reach the seventh…the fifth, sixth or seventh floor from the stairs, maybe the

fifth, but that's it. And then if you go down, (5)_____

_____ from here. You can't reach the other floors until you go down. So, until

you see the other side of building, you won't really (6)_____

_____. It's a very interesting, very, it's always, always is interesting, and will

continue to be interesting because of that. So a lot of interesting stuff.

Let's Write and Speak. ☺

5 Useful Expressions Step 1   CD 2-28

DVD の中に出てきた構文を使用した表現です。CD を聞いてリピーティングを行い、暗記するまで練習しましょう。

1. This building houses all of the arts.   （この建物は全ての芸術を収容している）

2. Until you see the other side, you won't really get a full picture.
                                  （反対側を見るまでは全体像をつかめないだろう）

6 **Writing and Speaking** Step 2

Useful Expressions を利用して、以下の下線に英語を入れて、自分の大学のことを話してみましょう。

1. This building _____.

2. Until you _____ you won't really _____.

7 **Writing and Speaking** Step 3

4のスクリプトを参考にして、自分自身の大学のことを話してみましょう。6で作成した英文も利用しましょう。

_____

_____

_____

_____

_____

Let's Read. ☺

8 **Key Words** Step 1

CD 2-29

Reading Passage に出てくる重要語を確認しましょう。選択欄から最も適切な日本語を選びましょう。また、CD を用いて発音の練習もしましょう。

1. endeavor _____
2. innovative _____
3. instill _____
4. mankind _____
5. empower _____
6. a broad array of _____
7. contemporary _____
8. brilliant _____
9. inspire _____
10. means _____
11. stimulate _____
12. unlock _____

人類	刺激する	引き出す	革新的な
手段	多岐にわたる	すばらしい	力を与える
鼓舞する	努力する	教え込む	現代の

次の英文は、ニューヨーク市立大学について説明しています。英文を速読して、以下の質問に、日本語で答えましょう。

Queens College focuses on the arts and humanities and we **endeavor** with our **innovative** curriculum not only to **instill** in students the three-thousand-year intellectual and cultural heritage of **mankind**, but to **empower** them to make their own creative contributions to that heritage. We offer **a broad array of** courses including languages and literature of **contemporary** Asia, the origins of the West in ancient Greece and Rome, the finest examples of the European and American novel, the treasures of world cinema, and linguistics. Moreover our **brilliant** teachers will **inspire** you with their own creative achievements. An Arts and Humanities education is the best path for exploring the intellectual life, not only as a historical heritage, but also as a **means** of **stimulating** your own creativity and **unlocking** your potential.

1. クイーンズ校ではどんな勉強に焦点を当てていますか。

　＿＿＿＿＿＿＿＿＿＿＿＿＿＿＿＿＿＿＿＿＿＿＿＿＿＿＿＿

2. まずどんなことを学生に教え込みますか。

　＿＿＿＿＿＿＿＿＿＿＿＿＿＿＿＿＿＿＿＿＿＿＿＿＿＿＿＿

3. 2の内容に加えて、どのような力を学生につけさせますか。

　＿＿＿＿＿＿＿＿＿＿＿＿＿＿＿＿＿＿＿＿＿＿＿＿＿＿＿＿

4. 具体的に、どんなコース科目を提供していますか。

　＿＿＿＿＿＿＿＿＿＿＿＿＿＿＿＿＿＿＿＿＿＿＿＿＿＿＿＿

5. すばらしい教員たちは、どうやって学生を鼓舞しますか。

　＿＿＿＿＿＿＿＿＿＿＿＿＿＿＿＿＿＿＿＿＿＿＿＿＿＿＿＿

6. 知的人生に導くものは何ですか。

　＿＿＿＿＿＿＿＿＿＿＿＿＿＿＿＿＿＿＿＿＿＿＿＿＿＿＿＿

Campus Tour (4):
City University of New York, Graduate Student

Let's Listen. ☺

1 Comprehension Step 1   *DVD* 25

ニューヨーク市立大学のキャンパスツアーの様子です。DVD を見て、以下の質問に日本語で答えましょう。

1. この部屋でどんなゲームやスポーツをして過ごすと言っていますか。2つ聞き取ってみましょう。

　_____

2. この部屋は、どれくらいの頻度で利用されると言っていますか。

　_____

2 Key Words Step 2   CD 2-31

DVD に出てきた重要語の確認をしましょう。選択欄から最も適切な日本語を選びましょう。また、CD を用いて発音の練習もしましょう。

1. self-esteem _____   2. pool _____

3. packed _____   4. simmer down _____

静まる	ビリヤード	自尊心	いっぱいである

3 Comprehension Step 2   *DVD* 25

重要語の確認ができたので、1回目よりは聞き取りやすくなっていると思います。それでは、もう一度 DVD を見て、もう少し細かな内容まで聞き取り、以下の質問に日本語で答えましょう。

1. Free hours の時間帯はいつですか。

　_____

2. どうして1の時間帯を Free hours と呼んでいるのですか。

　_____

3. Free hours のあとはどんな様子になると言っていますか。

　_____

CD を聞いて、下線部 (1) 〜 (8) の部分に英語を書き入れて、スクリプトを完成しましょう。スクリプトを完成したら、もう一度 DVD を見てみましょう。

Friend: Oh well, I, the Corner Pocket, um, I, I'm sorry, I feel a little nervous, but it's like a the Corner Pocket uh, so we just…work over here and uh, we just uh, play with later, can offer self-esteem for the day, um, we have some time to kind of (1)_____, so that's what kind of the Corner Pocket's for. Over here you can also do printing, as well as um, play other like (2)_____ _____, along with friends, uh, we (3)_____, we (4)_____, also…what else…we have…

Graduate Student: I mean how, how is the frequency the students here.

Friend: It's (5)_____, during free hour, it's…,

Graduate Student: Free hour, yeah.

Friend: It's packed.

Graduate Student: Free hours from (6)_____, so (7)_____. During that, that's why they call it Free Hours. So, everybody's free to do what they like.

Friend: Yeah, when it's um, when it's free hour it gets really packed. You get to not only, you know, play, but you also get uh, meet other people around here, it is really nice and engaging. And as well as, um, and after free hour let's if you don't wanna have to many…it's like, it all start to go sim, (8)_____, like late afternoon, you get to to just, enjoy a quick game before you go to a class…

Let's Write and Speak. ☺

5 Useful Expressions Step 1

CD 2-33

DVD の中に出てきた構文を使用した表現です。CD を聞いてリピーティングを行い、暗記するまで練習しましょう。

1. I have some time to enjoy swimming in the gym. （ジムで泳ぐ時間があります）

2. I always grab a shower before I go to a class. (授業に出る前にいつもシャワーを浴びます)

6 Writing and Speaking Step 2

Useful Expressions を利用して、以下の下線に英語を入れて、自分のことを話してみましょう。

1. I have some time to _____.

2. _____ before I go to _____.

7 Writing and Speaking Step 3

4のスクリプトを参考にして、自分自身の大学のことを話してみましょう。6で作成した英文も利用しましょう。

_____

_____

_____

_____

Let's Read. ☺

8 Key Words Step 1

CD 2-34

Reading Passage に出てくる重要語を確認しましょう。選択欄から最も適切な日本語を選びましょう。また、CD を用いて発音の練習もしましょう。

1. vibrant _____
2. metropolis _____
3. teeming _____
4. admission _____
5. renowned _____
6. sample _____
7. on exhibit _____
8. preeminent _____
9. flora _____
10. botanical garden _____
11. horizon _____
12. discovery _____

植物（相）	大変貴重な	大都市	展示（公開）されて
有名な	植物園	活力に満ちた	経験して知る
入場料	溢れている	発見	視野

9 Reading Step 2

次の英文は、ニューヨーク市立大学について説明しています。英文を速読して、以下の質問に、日本語で答えましょう。

New York City is a **vibrant metropolis** with a **teeming** intellectual and cultural life and as a CUNY student, you can get free or discount **admission** to many of the city's most **renowned** sites. CUNY also offers a Cultural Passport which provides all students, staff, and faculty with access to a wide variety of the city's most exciting spots. With the passport, you have the run of one of the world's most exciting cities, and admission is either free or discounted. The Cultural Passport enables you to **sample** not only the world-famous theater attractions staged each night on Broadway, but also the artistic and cultural treasures **on exhibit** at some of the world's **preeminent** museums, as well as the **flora** on display at New York's outdoor **botanical gardens**. Broaden your intellectual **horizons** with this priceless opportunity for **discovery!**

1. ニューヨーク市はどんな街ですか。

_____

2. Cultural Passport を使うことができるのは、どのような人ですか。

_____

3. Cultural Passport を持っていると、どんな優遇を受けることができますか。

_____

4. Cultural Passport はどんな場所で使うことができますか。

_____

5. 最後にこの機会を利用して、どんなことをしてほしいとアドバイスしていますか。

_____

City University of New York, Queens College Campus (Powdermaker Hall)

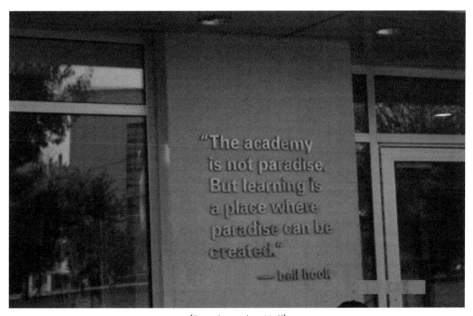

(Powdermaker Hall)

(Klapper Hall)

(Rosenthal Library)

音声ファイルのダウンロード方法

英宝社ホームページ（http://www.eihosha.co.jp/）の
「テキスト音声ダウンロード」バナーをクリックすると、
音声ファイルダウンロードページにアクセスできます。

Talking About Our Campus
映像で巡る海外のキャンパス

2021年1月15日　初　版　　　　　　　　2023年10月20日　第2刷

編　著　者ⓒ　小笠原　真　司
奥　田　阿　子
COLLINS William
廣　江　　　顕
木　戸　康　人

発　行　者　佐　々　木　　　元

発　行　所　株式会社　英　　宝　　社
〒101-0032 東京都千代田区岩本町2-7-7
Tel［03］(5833) 5870　Fax［03］(5833) 5872

ISBN978-4-269-41041-1 C1082
［製版：㈱マナ・コムレード／表紙デザイン：伊谷企画／印刷・製本：モリモト印刷㈱］